C000156007

LOVE
POEMS

LOVE POEMS

First published in 2001 as *Classic Love Poems*
Reprinted 2005/ Second edition published in 2006/ Third edition published in 2008/ Fourth edition published in 2014
This revised edition copyright © Summersdale Publishers Ltd, 2016

Summersdale Publishers Ltd
46 West Street
Chichester
West Sussex
PO19 1RP
UK

www.summersdale.com

Printed and bound in the Czech Republic

ISBN: 978-1-84953-804-6

Substantial discounts on bulk quantities of Summersdale books are available to corporations, professional associations and other organisations. For details contact Nicky Douglas by telephone: +44 (0) 1243 756902, fax: +44 (0) 1243 786300 or email: nicky@summersdale.com.

LOVE
POEMS

EDITED BY
MAX MORRIS

summersdale

CONTENTS

INTRODUCTION

Some poems yearn and hope and despair, some rejoice and crow that they've found their soulmate and their heart's partner. Some are polished displays of skill and virtuosity, some seem as if the words were wrested from poet's pen. The very best love poetry beats in time with your heart and makes you marvel that, even separated by years and continents, there is someone out there who has loved in the way that you love. Although the poets in this collection are long gone, their words of passion, infatuation, longing and tenderness have survived through the years to speak from these pages. Love and poetry can immortalise, and as Shakespeare wrote:

So long as men can breathe, or eyes can see,
So long lives this, and this gives life to thee.

If I had the talent of Valmiki
I would write a poem
with my lover as heroine.
The first ten parts would be given
over to the ten fingers of her hands,
for they wove a veil in which
I have wrapped up all
my ancient loves.
And I would consecrate
the ten others
to the ten nights we spent
at Mabhahat.

AMARU

Over the reeds the
Twilight mists rise and settle.
The wild ducks cry out
As the evening turns cold.
Lover, how I long for you.

ANONYMOUS FRONTIER GUARD,
MANYOSHU

OYAKEME, A GIRL OF BUZEN

In the dusk
The road is hard to see.
Wait 'till moonrise,
So I can watch you go.

ANONYMOUS

THE DREAM

All trembling in my arms Aminta lay,
Defending of the bliss I strove to take;
Raising my rapture by her kind delay,
Her force so charming was and weak.
The soft resistance did betray the grant,
While I pressed on the heaven of my desires;
Her rising breasts with nimbler motions pant;
Her dying eyes assume new fires.
Now to the height of languishment she grows,
And still her looks new charms put on;
Now the last mystery of Love she knows,
We sigh, and kiss: I waked, and all was done.

'Twas but a dream, yet by my heart I knew,
Which still was panting, part of it was true:
Oh how I strove the rest to have believed;
Ashamed and angry to be undeceived!

APHRA BEHN

THE QUESTION ANSWERED

What is it men in women do require?
 The lineaments of Gratified Desire.
What is it women do in men require?
 The lineaments of Gratified Desire.

WILLIAM BLAKE

LOVE'S SECRET

Never seek to tell thy love
Love that never told can be;
For the gentle wind does move
Silently, invisibly.

I told my love, I told my love,
I told her all my heart,
Trembling, cold, in ghastly fears –
Ah! she doth depart.

Soon as she was gone from me,
A traveller came by,
Silently, invisibly:
He took her with a sigh.

WILLIAM BLAKE

A LETTER TO HER HUSBAND, ABSENT UPON PUBLICK EMPLOYMENT

My head, my heart, mine Eyes, my life, nay more,
My joy, my Magazine of earthly store,
If two be one, as surely thou and I,
How stayest thou there, whilst I at Ipswich lye?
So many steps, head from the heart to sever
If but a neck, soon should we be together:
I like the earth this season, mourn in black,
My Sun is gone so far in's Zodiack,
Whom whilst I 'joy'd, nor storms, nor frosts I felt,
His warmth such frigid colds did cause to melt.
My chilled limbs now nummed lye forlorn;

Return, return sweet Sol from Capricorn;
In this dead time, alas, what can I more
Then view those fruits which through thy heat I bore?
Which sweet contentment yield me for a space,
True living Pictures of their Fathers face.
O strange effect! now thou art *Southward* gone,
I weary grow, the tedious day so long;
But when thou *Northward* to me shalt return,
I wish my Sun may never set, but burn
Within the Cancer of my glowing breast,
The welcome house of him my dearest guest.
Where ever, ever stay, and go not thence,
Till natures sad decree shall call thee hence;
Flesh of thy flesh, bone of thy bone,
I here, thou there, yet both but one.

ANNE BRADSTREET

TO MY DEAR AND LOVING HUSBAND

If ever two were one, then surely we;
If ever man were lov'd by wife, then thee;
If ever wife was happy in a man,
Compare with me, ye women, if you can.
I prize thy love more than whole Mines of gold,
Or all the riches that the East doth hold.
My love is such that Rivers cannot quench,
Nor aught but love from thee, give recompence.
Thy love is such I can no way repay;
The heavens reward thee manifold, I pray.
Then while we live in love let's so perséver
That when we live no more we may live ever.

ANNE BRADSTREET

from SILENT IS THE HOUSE

Come, the wind may never again
Blow as it now blows for us;
And the stars may never again
shine as now they shine:
Long before October returns,
Seas of blood will have parted us;
And you must crush the love in
your heart,
and I the love in mine!

EMILY BRONTË

SONNETS FROM THE PORTUGUESE XLIII

How do I love thee? Let me count the ways.
I love thee to the depth and breadth and height
My soul can reach, when feeling out of sight
For the ends of Being and ideal Grace.
I love thee to the level of everyday's
Most quiet need, by sun and candle-light.
I love thee freely, as men strive for Right;
I love thee purely, as they turn from Praise.
I love thee with the passion put to use

In my old griefs, and with my childhood's faith.
I love thee with a love I seemed to lose
With my lost saints, – I love thee with the breath,
Smiles, tears, of all my life! – and, if God choose,
I shall but love thee better after death.

ELIZABETH BARRETT BROWNING

SONNETS FROM
THE PORTUGUESE X

Yet, love, mere love, is beautiful indeed
And worthy of acceptation. Fire is bright,
Let temple burn, or flax; an equal light
Leaps in the flame from cedar-plank or weed.
And love is fire. And when I say at need
I love thee… mark!… I love thee – in thy sight
I stand transfigured, glorified aright,
With conscience of the new rays that proceed
Out of my face toward thine. There's nothing low
In love, when love the lowest: meanest creatures
Who love God, God accepts while loving so.
And what I *feel*, across the inferior features
Of what I *am*, doth flash itself, and show
How that great work of Love enhances Nature's.

ELIZABETH BARRETT BROWNING

SONNETS FROM THE PORTUGUESE XII

Indeed this very love which is my boast,
And which, when rising up from breast to brow,
Doth crown me with a ruby large enow
To draw men's eyes and prove the inner cost,
This love even, all my worth, to the uttermost,
I should not love withal, unless that thou
Hadst set me an example, shown me how,
When first thine earnest eyes with mine were crossed,
And love called love. And thus, I cannot speak
Of love even, as a good thing of my own.
Thy soul hath snatched up mine all faint and weak,
And placed it by thee on a golden throne,—
And that I love (O soul, we must be meek!)
Is by thee only, whom I love alone.

ELIZABETH BARRETT BROWNING

SONNETS FROM THE PORTUGUESE XX

Belovèd, my Belovèd, when I think
That thou wast in the world a year ago,
What time I sat alone here in the snow
And saw no footprint, heard the silence sink
No moment at thy voice, but, link by link,
Went counting all my chains as if that so
They never could fall off at any blow
Struck by thy possible hand – why, thus I drink
Of life's great cup of wonder! Wonderful,
Never to feel thee thrill the day or night
With personal act or speech, – nor even cull
Some prescience of thee with the blossoms white
Thou sawest growing! Atheists are as dull,
Who cannot guess God's presence out of sight.

ELIZABETH BARRETT BROWNING

SONNETS FROM
THE PORTUGUESE XIII

And wilt thou have me fashion into speech
The love I bear thee, finding words enough,
And hold the torch out, while the winds are rough
Between our faces, to cast light on each? –
I drop it at thy feet. I cannot teach
My hand to hold my spirit so far off
From myself – me – that I should bring thee proof
In words, of love hid in me out of reach.
Nay, let the silence of my womanhood
Commend my woman-love to thy belief, –
Seeing that I stand unwon, however wooed,
And rend the garment of my life, in brief,
By a most dauntless, voiceless fortitude,
Lest one touch of this heart convey its grief.

ELIZABETH BARRETT BROWNING

SONNETS FROM
THE PORTUGUESE XXXV

If I leave all for thee, wilt thou exchange
And be all to me? Shall I never miss
Home-talk and blessing and the common kiss
That comes to each in turn, nor count it strange,
When I look up, to drop on a new range
Of walls and floors, another home than this?
Nay, wilt thou fill that place by me which is
Filled by dead eyes too tender to know change?
That's hardest. If to conquer love, has tried,
To conquer grief, tries more, as all things prove
For grief indeed is love and grief beside.
Alas, I have grieved so I am hard to love.
Yet love me – wilt thou? Open thine heart wide,
And fold within the wet wings of thy dove.

ELIZABETH BARRETT BROWNING

IN A GONDOLA

The moth's kiss, first!
Kiss me as if you made believe
You were not sure, this eve,
How my face, your flower, had pursed
Its petals up; so, here and there
You brush it, till I grow aware
Who wants me, and wide ope I burst.

The bee's kiss, now!
Kiss me as if you enter'd gay
My heart at some noonday,
A bud that dares not disallow
The claim, so all is render'd up,
And passively its shatter'd cup
Over your head to sleep I bow.

ROBERT BROWNING

A RED RED ROSE

O my Luve is like a red, red rose,
That's newly sprung in June:
O my Luve is like the melodie
That's sweetly play'd in tune.

As fair art thou, my bonie lass,
So deep in luve am I,
And I will luve thee still, my Dear,
Till a' the seas gang dry.

Till a' the seas gang dry, my Dear,
And the rocks melt wi' the sun!
I will luve thee still, my Dear,
While the sands o' life shall run.

And fare-thee-weel, my only Luve!
And fare-thee-weel, a while!
And I will come again, my Luve,
Tho' it were ten-thousand mile!

ROBERT BURNS

I LOVE MY JEAN

Of a' the airts the wind can blaw,
I dearly like the west,
For there the bonie Lassie lives,
The Lassie I lo'e best:
There wild woods grow, and rivers row,
And mony a hill' between;
But day and night my fancy's flight
Is ever wi' my Jean.

I see her in the dewy flowers,
I see her sweet and fair;
I hear her in the tunefu' birds
I hear her charm the air:
There's not a bonie flower that springs
By fountain, shaw, or green;
There's not a bonie bird that sings
But minds me o' my Jean.

ROBERT BURNS

HAD I A CAVE

Had I a cave on some wild, distant shore,
Where the winds howl to the waves' dashing roar,
There would I weep my woes,
There seek my lost repose,
Till grief my eyes should close,
Ne'er to wake more!

Falsest of womankind, can'st thou declare
All thy fond-plighted vows – fleeting as air!
To thy new lover hie,
Laugh o'er thy perjury;
Then in thy bosom try
What peace is there!

ROBERT BURNS

SHE WALKS IN BEAUTY

She walks in Beauty, like the night
Of cloudless climes and starry skies;
And all that's best of dark and bright
Meet in her aspect and her eyes:
Thus mellowed to that tender light
Which Heaven to gaudy day denies.

One shade the more, one ray the less,
Had half impaired the nameless grace
Which waves in every raven tress,
Or softly lightens o'er her face;
Where thoughts serenely sweet express
How pure, how dear their dwelling-place.

And on that cheek, and o'er that brow,
So soft, so calm, yet eloquent,
The smiles that win, the tints that glow,
But tell of days in goodness spent,
A mind at peace with all below,
A heart whose love is innocent!

LORD BYRON

OH! SNATCHED AWAY IN BEAUTY'S BLOOM

Oh! snatched away in Beauty's bloom,
On thee shall press no ponderous tomb;
But on thy turf shall roses rear
Their leaves, the earliest of the year;
And the wild cypress wave in tender gloom:

And oft by yon blue gushing stream
Shall Sorrow lean her drooping head,
And feed deep thought with many a dream,
And lingering pause and lightly tread;
Fond wretch! as if her step disturbed the dead!

Away! we know that tears are vain,
That Death nor heeds nor hears distress:
Will this unteach us to complain?
Or make one mourner weep the less?
And thou – who tell'st me to forget
Thy looks are wan, thine eyes are wet.

LORD BYRON

STANZAS FOR MUSIC

There be none of Beauty's daughters
With a magic like thee;
And like music on the waters
Is thy sweet voice to me:
When, as if its sound were causing
The charmèd Ocean's pausing,
The waves lie still and gleaming,
And the lull'd winds seem dreaming.

And the Midnight Moon is weaving
Her bright chain o'er the deep;
Whose breast is gently heaving,
As an infant's asleep:
So the spirit bows before thee,
To listen and adore thee;
With a full but soft emotion,
Like the swell of Summer's ocean.

LORD BYRON

TO ELLEN

Oh! might I kiss those eyes of fire,
A million scarce would quench desire:
Still would I steep my lips in bliss,
And dwell an age on every kiss;
Nor then my soul should sated be,
Still would I kiss and cling to thee:
Nought should my kiss from thine dissever;
Still would we kiss, and kiss forever,
E'en though the numbers did exceed
The yellow harvest's countless seed.
To part would be a vain endeavor:
Could I desist? – ah! never – never!

LORD BYRON

CHERRY RIPE

There is a garden in her face,
    Where roses and white lilies grow;
A heavenly paradise is that place,
    Wherein all pleasant fruits do grow;
There cherries grow which none may buy,
Till Cherry-ripe themselves do cry.

Those cherries fairly do enclose
    Of orient pearl a double row,
Which when her lovely laughter shows,
    They look like rosebuds fill'd with snow;
Yet them no peer nor prince can buy
Till Cherry-ripe themselves do cry.

Her eyes like angels watch them still;
Her brows like bended bows do stand,
Threatening with piercing frowns to kill
All that attempt with eye or hand
Those sacred cherries to come nigh,
Till Cherry-ripe themselves do cry.

THOMAS CAMPION

MY LADY'S EYES

Mistress, since you so much desire
To know the place of Cupid's fire
In your fair shrine that flame doth rest,
Yet never harboured in your breast.

It bides not in your lips so sweet,
Nor where the rose and lilies meet;
But a little higher, a little higher,
There, there, O there lies Cupid's fire.

Even in those starry piercing eyes,
There Cupid's sacred fire lies;
Those eyes I strive not to enjoy,
For they have power to destroy:

Nor woo I for a smile or kiss,
So meanly triumphs not my bliss;
But a little higher, a little higher
I climb to crown my chaste desire.

THOMAS CAMPION

MY LIFE'S DELIGHT

Come, O come, my life's delight,
Let me not in languor pine!
Love loves no delay; thy sight,
The more enjoyed, the more divine:
O come, and take from me
The pain of being deprived of thee!

Thou all sweetness dost enclose,
Like a little world of bliss.
Beauty guards thy looks: the rose
In them pure and eternal is.
Come, then, and make thy flight
As swift to me, as heavenly light.

THOMAS CAMPION

RED AND WHITE ROSES

Read in these Roses the sad story
Of my hard fate, and your owne glory.
In the White you may discover
The paleness of a fainting lover;
In the Red, the flames still feeding
On my heart, with fresh wounds bleeding.
The White will tell you how I languish,
And the Red express my anguish;
The White my innocence displaying,
The Red my martyrdom betraying.
The frowns that on your brow resided,
Have those Roses thus divided.
Oh! let your smiles but clear the weather,
And then they both shall grow together.

THOMAS CAREW

SONG: MEDIOCRITY IN LOVE REJECTED

Give me more love or more disdain;
The torrid or the frozen zone
Bring equal ease unto my pain,
The temperate affords me none:
Either extreme of love or hate,
Is sweeter than a calm estate.

Give me a storm; if it be love,
Like Danaë in that golden shower,
I swim in pleasure; if it prove
Disdain, that torrent will devour
My vulture hopes; and he's possess'd
Of heaven, that's but from hell releas'd.
Then crown my joys or cure my pain:
Give me more love or more disdain.

THOMAS CAREW

from TO CHLOE, WHO FOR HIS SAKE WISHED HERSELF YOUNGER

There are two Births; the one when Light
    First strikes the new awaken'd sense;
    The Other when two Souls unite,
And we must count our life from thence:
    When you lov'd me and I lov'd you
    The both of us were born anew.

Love then to us new Souls did give
    And in those Souls did plant new pow'rs;
    Since when another life we live,
The Breath we breathe is his, not ours:
Love makes those young whom Age doth Chill,
    And whom he finds young keeps young still.

WILLIAM CARTWRIGHT

HOW MANY KISSES: TO LESBIA

Lesbia, you ask how many kisses of yours
would be enough and more to satisfy me.
As many as the grains of Libyan sand
that lie between hot Jupiter's oracle,
at Ammon, in resin-producing Cyrene,
and old Battiades sacred tomb:
or as many as the stars, when night is still,
gazing down on secret human desires:
as many of your kisses kissed
are enough, and more, for mad Catullus,
as can't be counted by spies
nor an evil tongue bewitch us.

CATULLUS

LET'S LIVE AND LOVE: TO LESBIA

Let us live, my Lesbia and let us love,
and all the words of the old, and so moral,
may they be worth less than nothing to us!
Suns may set, and suns may rise again:
but when our brief light has set,
night is one long everlasting sleep.

Give me a thousand kisses, a hundred more,
another thousand, and another hundred,
and, when we've counted up the many thousands,
confuse them so as not to know them all,
so that no enemy may cast an evil eye,
by knowing that there were so many kisses.

CATALLUS

LOVE'S PAINS

This love, I canna' bear it,
It cheats me night and day;
This love, I canna' wear it
It takes my peace away.

This love, wa' once a flower;
But now it is a thorn—
The joy o' evening hour,
Turn'd to a pain e're morn.

This love, it wa' a bud,
And a secret known to me;
Like a flower within a wood;
Like a nest within a tree.

This love, wrong understood,
Oft' turned my joy to pain;
I tried to throw away the bud,
But the blossom would remain.

JOHN CLARE

49

SONG

I wish I was where I would be
With love alone to dwell;
Was I but her or she but me
Then love would all be well.
I wish to send my thoughts to her
As quick as thoughts can fly;
But as the winds the waters stir
The mirrors change and flye.

JOHN CLARE

LOVE'S MEMORIES

Love's memories haunt my footsteps still
Like ceaseless flowings of the river.
Its mystic depths say what can fill?
Sad disappointment waits forever.

JOHN CLARE

THE EXCHANGE

We pledged our hearts, my love and I,
   I in my arms the maiden clasping;
   I could not guess the reason why,
But, Oh! I trembled like an aspen.

   Her father's love she bade me gain;
   I went, but shook like any reed!
   I strove to act the man – in vain!
We had exchanged our hearts indeed.

SAMUEL TAYLOR COLERIDGE

from ON MRS ARABELLA HUNT SINGING

Let all be husht, each softer Motion cease,
Be ev'ry loud tumultuous Thought at Peace,
And ev'ry ruder Gasp of Breath
Be calm, as in the Arms of Death.
And thou most fickle, most uneasie Part,
Thou restless Wanderer, my Heart,
Be still; gently, ah gently, leave,
Thou busie, idle thing, to heave.
Stir not a Pulse; and let my Blood,
That turbulent, unruly Flood,
Be softly staid:
Let me be all, but my Attention, dead.
Go, rest, y'unnecessary Springs of Life,
Leave your officious Toil and Strife;
For I would hear her Voice, and try
If it be possible to die.

WILLIAM CONGREVE

SONNET

My lady's presence makes the Roses red
Because to see her lips they blush for shame;
The Lily's leaves, for envy, pale became,
For her white hands in them this envy bred.
The Marigold the leaves abroad doth spread,
Because the sun's and her power is the same
The Violet of purple colour came,
Dyed in the blood she made my heart to shed.
In brief, all flowers from her their virtue take;
From her sweet breath their sweet smells do proceed;
The living heat which her eyebeams doth make
Warmeth the ground, and quickeneth the seed.
The rain, wherewith she watereth the flowers,
Falls from mine eyes, which she dissolves in showers.

HENRY CONSTABLE

HIS MOTHER'S WEDDING RING

The ring, so worn as you behold,
So thin, so pale, is yet of gold:
The passion such it was to prove—
Worn with life's cares, love yet was love.

GEORGE CRABBE

THAT I DID ALWAYS LOVE

That I did always love,
I bring thee proof:
That till I loved
I did not love enough.

That I shall love alway,
I offer thee
That love is life,
And life hath immortality.

This, dost thou doubt, sweet?
Then have I
Nothing to show
But Calvary

EMILY DICKINSON

from THE ANNIVERSARY

All other things to their
destruction draw,
Only our love hath no decay;
This, no tomorrow hath,
nor yesterday,
Running it never runs from
us away,
But truly keeps his first, last,
everlasting day.

JOHN DONNE

AIR AND ANGELS

Twice or thrice had I lov'd thee,
Before I knew thy face or name;
So in a voice, so in a shapeless flame
Angels affect us oft, and worship'd be;
Still when, to where thou wert, I came,
Some lovely glorious nothing I did see.
But since my soul, whose child love is,
Takes limbs of flesh, and else could nothing do,
More subtle than the parent is
Love must not be, but take a body too;
And therefore what thou wert, and who,
I bid Love ask, and now
That it assume thy body, I allow,
And fix itself in thy lip, eye, and brow.

Whilst thus to ballast love, I thought,
And so more steadily to have gone,
With wares which would sink admiration,
I saw I had love's pinnace overfraught;
Ev'ry thy hair for love to work upon
Is much too much, some fitter must be sought;
For, nor in nothing, nor in things
Extreme, and scatt'ring bright, can love inhere;
Then, as an angel, face, and wings
Of air, not pure as it, yet pure, doth wear,
So thy love may be my love's sphere;
Just such disparity
As is 'twixt air and angels' purity,
'Twixt women's love, and men's, will ever be.

JOHN DONNE

TO A LADY ASKING HIM HOW LONG HE WOULD LOVE HER

It is not, Celia, in our power
To say how long our love will last;
It may be we within this hour
May lose those joys we now do taste:
The blessèd, that immortal be,
From change in love are only free.

Then since we mortal lovers are,
Ask not how long our love will last;
But while it does, let us take care
Each minute be with pleasure past:
Were it not madness to deny
To live because we're sure to die?

GEORGE ETHEREDGE

TO ELECTRA

I dare not ask a kiss,
I dare not beg a smile,
Lest having that, or this,
I might grow proud the while.

No, no, the utmost share
Of my desire shall be,
Only to kiss that air,
That lately kissèd thee.

ROBERT HERRICK

TO THE VIRGINS,
TO MAKE MUCH OF TIME

Gather ye Rose-buds while ye may,
    Old Time is still a-flying:
And this same flower that smiles today
    Tomorrow will be dying.

The glorious Lamp of Heaven, the Sun,
    The higher he's a-getting,
The sooner will his Race be run
    And nearer he's to Setting.

That Age is best, which is the first,
When Youth and Blood are warmer;
But being spent, the worse, and worst
Times still succeed the former.

Then be not coy, but use your time,
And while ye may, go marry:
For having lost but once your prime,
You may for ever tarry.

ROBERT HERRICK

UPON THE NIPPLES OF JULIA'S BREAST

Have ye beheld (with much delight)
A red-rose peeping through a white?
Or else a cherry (double grac'd)
Within a lillie? Centre plac'd?
Or ever mark'd the pretty beam,
A strawberry shewes, halfe drown'd in cream?
Or seen rich rubies blushing through
A pure smooth pearl, and Orient too?
So like to this, nay all the rest,
Is each neat niplet of her breast.

ROBERT HERRICK

UPON JULIA'S CLOTHES

When as in silks my Julia goes,
Then, then (me thinks) how sweetly flowes
The liquefaction of her clothes.

Next, when I cast mine eyes and see
That brave vibration each way free,
O how that glittering taketh me!

ROBERT HERRICK

Your hair has turned white
While your heart stayed
Knotted against me.
I shall never
Loosen it now.

KAKINOMOTO NO HITOMARO

THE TIME OF ROSES

It was not in the Winter
Our loving lot was cast;
It was the Time of Roses—
We pluck'd them as we pass'd!

[...]

'Twas twilight, and I bade you go,
But still you held me fast;
It was the Time of Roses—
We pluck'd them as we pass'd!

What else could peer thy glowing cheek,
That tears began to stud?
And when I ask'd the like of Love
You snatch'd a damask bud;

And oped it to the dainty core,
Still glowing to the last;
It was the Time of Roses—
We pluck'd them as we pass'd!

THOMAS HOOD

I LOVE THEE

I love thee – I love thee!
'Tis all that I can say;
It is my vision in the night,
My dreaming in the day;
The very echo of my heart,
The blessing when I pray.
I love thee – I love thee!

I love thee – I love thee!
Is ever on my tongue.
In all my proudest poesy
That chorus still is sung;
It is the verdict of my eyes
Amidst the gay and young:
I love thee – I love thee!
A thousand maids among.

I love thee – I love thee!
Thy bright and hazel glance,
The mellow lute upon those lips,
Whose tender tones entrance.
But most, dear heart of hearts,
thy proofs.
That still these words enhance!
I love thee – I love thee!
Whatever be thy chance.

THOMAS HOOD

ONLY WE

Dream no more that grief and pain
Could such hearts as ours enchain,
Safe from loss and safe from gain,
    Free, as Love makes free.

When false friends pass coldly by,
    Sigh, in earnest pity, sigh,
Turning thine unclouded eye
    Up from them to me.

Hear not danger's trampling feet
Feel not sorrow's wintry sleet
Trust that life is just and meet,
With mine arm round Thee.

Lip on lip, and eye to eye,
Love to love, we live, we die;
No more Thou, and no more I,
We, and only We!

RICHARD MONCKTON MILNES,
LORD HOUGHTON

MORE STRONG THAN TIME

Since I have set my lips to your full cup, my sweet,
Since I my pallid face between your hands have laid,
Since I have known your soul, and all the bloom of it,
And all the perfume rare, now buried in the shade;

Since it was given to me to hear on happy while,
The words wherein your heart spoke all its mysteries,
Since I have seen you weep, and since I have
seen you smile,
Your lips upon my lips, and your eyes
upon my eyes;

Since I have known above my forehead
glance and gleam,
A ray, a single ray, of your star, veiled always,
Since I have felt the fall, upon my lifetime's stream,
Of one rose petal plucked from the roses of your days;

I now am bold to say to the swift changing hours,
Pass, pass upon your way, for I grow never old,
Fleet to the dark abysm with all your fading flowers,
One rose that none may pluck, within my heart I hold.

Your flying wings may smite, but they can never spill
The cup fulfilled of love, from which my lips are wet;
My heart has far more fire than you can frost to chill,
My soul more love than you can make my soul forget.

VICTOR HUGO

BOAZ ASLEEP

Boaz, overcome with weariness, by torchlight
    made his pallet on the threshing floor
      where all day he had worked, and
        now he slept
    among the bushels of threshed wheat.

The old man owned wheatfields and barley,
    and though he was rich, he was
      still fair-minded.
No filth soured the sweetness of his well.
No hot iron of torture whitened in his forge.

His beard was silver as a brook in April.
He bound sheaves without the strain of hate
or envy. He saw gleaners pass, and said,
Let handfuls of the fat ears fall to them.

The man's mind, clear of untoward feeling,
clothed itself in candor. He wore clean robes.
His heaped granaries spilled over always
toward the poor, no less than public fountains.

Boaz did well by his workers and by kinsmen.
He was generous, and moderate. Women held him
worthier than younger men, for
youth is handsome,
but to him in his old age came greatness.

An old man, nearing his first source, may find
the timelessness beyond times of trouble.
And though fire burned in young men's eyes,
to Ruth the eyes of Boaz shone clear light.

VICTOR HUGO

RONDEAU

Jenny kiss'd me when we met,
Jumping from the chair she sat in;
Time, you thief, who love to get
Sweets into your list, put that in!
Say I'm weary, say I'm sad,
Say that health and wealth have miss'd me,
Say I'm growing old, but add,
Jenny kiss'd me.

LEIGH HUNT

TO CELIA

Drink to me, only, with thine eyes,
And I will pledge with mine;
Or leave a kiss but in the cup
And I'll not look for wine.
The thirst that from the soul doth rise
Doth ask a drink divine;
But might I of Jove's nectar sup
I would not change for thine.

I sent thee late a rosy wreath,
Not so much honouring thee
As giving it a hope, that there
It could not wither'd be;
But thou thereon did'st only breathe
And sent'st it back to me;
Since when it grows, and smells, I swear,
Not of itself, but thee!

BEN JONSON

A VISION OF BEAUTY

It was a beauty that I saw—
So pure, so perfect, as the frame
Of all the universe were lame
To that one figure, could I draw,
Or give least line of it a law:
A skein of silk without a knot!
A fair march made without a halt!
A curious form without a fault!
A printed book without a blot!
All beauty! – and without a spot.

BEN JONSON

SONG

Have you seen but a bright lily grow
Before rude hands have touch'd it?
Have you mark'd but the fall of
the snow
Before the soil has smutch'd it?
Have you felt the wool of beaver,
Or swan's down ever?
Or gave smelt o' the bud o' the brier,
Or the nard in the fire?
Or have ever tasted the bag of
the bee?
O so white, O so soft, O so sweet
is she!

BEN JONSON

THOSE EYES

Oh! do not wanton with those eyes,
Lest I be sick with seeing—
Nor cast them down, but let them rise,
Lest shame destroy their being.

Oh! be not angry with those fires,
For then their threats will kill me;
Nor look too kind on my desires,
For then my hopes will spill me.

Oh! do not steep them in thy tears,
For so will sorrow slay me;
Nor spread them as distraught with fears—
Mine own enough betray me.

BEN JONSON

SONNET XX

Bright star, would I were stedfast as thou art—
Not in lone splendour hung aloft the night
And watching, with eternal lids apart,
Like nature's patient, sleepless Eremite,
The moving waters at their priestlike task
Of pure ablution round earth's human shores,
Or gazing on the new soft-fallen mask
Of snow upon the mountains and the moors—
No – yet still stedfast, still unchangeable,
Pillow'd upon my fair love's ripening breast,
To feel forever its soft fall and swell,
Awake forever in a sweet unrest,
Still, still to hear her tender-taken breath,
And so live ever – or else swoon to death.

JOHN KEATS

SONNET XIX
TO FANNY

I cry your mercy – pity – love! – ay, love!—
　Merciful love that tantalises not,
One-thoughted, never-wandering, guileless love,
　Unmask'd, and being seen – without a blot!
O! let me have thee whole – all – all – be mine!
That shape, that fairness, that sweet minor zest
Of love, your kiss – those hands, those eyes divine,
That warm, white, lucent, million-pleasured breast—
　Yourself – your soul – in pity give me all,
　Withhold no atom's atom or I die,
　Or living on perhaps, your wretched thrall,
　　Forget, in the midst of idle misery,
　Life's purposes – the palate of my mind
　Losing its gust, and my ambition blind!

JOHN KEATS

THE EVENING STAR

Lo! in the painted oriel of the West,
Whose panes the sunken sun incarnadines,
Like a fair lady at her casement, shines
The evening star, the star of love and rest!
And then anon she doth herself divest
Of all her radiant garments, and reclines
Behind the sombre screen of yonder pines,
With slumber and soft dreams of love oppressed.
O my beloved, my sweet Hesperus!
My morning and my evening star of love!
My best and gentlest lady! even thus,
As that fair planet in the sky above,
Dost thou retire unto thy rest at night,
And from thy darkened window fades the light.

HENRY WADSWORTH LONGFELLOW

from DOCTOR FAUSTUS

Was this the face that launch'd a thousand ships
And burnt the topless towers of Ilium?
Sweet Helen, make me immortal with a kiss:
Her lips suck forth my soul – see where it flies!
Come, Helen, come, give me my soul again.
Here will I dwell, for heaven is in these lips
And all is dross that is not Helena.
I will be Paris, and for love of thee
Instead of Troy shall Wittenberg be sack'd,
And I will combat with weak Menelaus,
And wear thy colours on my plumèd crest:
Yea, I will wound Achilles in the heel,
And then return to Helen for a kiss.

O, thou art fairer than the evening's air,
Clad in the beauty of a thousand stars!
Brighter art thou than flaming Jupiter,
When he appear'd to hapless Semele:
More lovely than the monarch of the sky
In wanton Arethusa's azur'd arms,
And none but thou shalt be my paramour!

CHRISTOPHER MARLOWE

WHEN I WOULD IMAGE

When I would image her features,
   Comes up a shrouded head:
I touch the outlines, shrinking;
She seems of the wandering dead.

But when love asks for nothing,
   And lies on his bed of snow,
The face slips under my eyelids,
   All in its living glow.

Like a dark cathedral city,
Whose spires, and domes, and towers
Quiver in violet lightnings,
   My soul basks on for hours.

GEORGE MEREDITH

from LOVE IN THE VALLEY

Soft new beech-leaves, up to beamy April
Spreading bough on bough a primrose
mountain, you,
Lucid in the moon, raise lilies to the skyfields,
Youngest green transfused in silver shining through:
Fairer than the lily, than the wild white cherry:
Fair as in image my seraph love appears
Borne to me by dreams when dawn is at my eyelids:
Fair as in the flesh she swims to me on tears.

Could I find a place to be alone with heaven,
I would speak my heart out: heaven is my need.
Every woodland tree is flushing like the dog-wood,
Flashing like the whitebeam, swaying like the reed.
Flushing like the dog-wood crimson in October;
Streaming like the flag-reed South-West blown;
Flashing as in gusts the sudden-lighted white beam:
All seem to know what is for heaven alone.

GEORGE MEREDITH

from PARADISE LOST BOOK IV

With thee conversing I forget all time,
All seasons and their change, all please alike.
Sweet is the breath of morn, her rising sweet,
With charm of earliest birds; pleasant the sun
When first on this delightful land he spreads
His orient beams, on herb, tree, fruit, and flow'r,
Glist'ring with dew; fragrant the fertile earth

After soft showers; and sweet the coming on
Of grateful ev'ning mild, then silent night
With this her solemn bird and this fair moon,
And these the gems of heav'n, her starry train:
But neither breath of morn when she ascends
With charm of earliest birds, nor rising sun

On this delightful land, nor herb, fruit, flow'r,
Glist'ring with dew, nor fragrance after showers,
Nor grateful ev'ning mild, nor silent night
With this her solemn bird, nor walk by moon,
Or glittering starlight without thee is sweet.

JOHN MILTON

THE MONOPOLIST

If I were yonder wave, my dear,
And thou the isle it clasps around,
I would not let a foot come near
My land of bliss, my fairy ground!

If I were yonder conch of gold,
And thou the pearl within it placed,
I would not let an eye behold
The sacred gem my arms embraced!

If I were yonder orange tree,
And thou the blossom blooming there,
I would not yield a breath of thee,
To scent the most imploring air!

THOMAS MOORE

BELIEVE ME, IF ALL THOSE ENDEARING YOUNG CHARMS

Believe me, if all those endearing young charms,
Which I gaze on so fondly to-day,
Were to change by to-morrow, and fleet in my arms,
Like fairy-gifts fading away!
Thou wouldst still be ador'd, as this moment thou art,
Let thy loveliness fade as it will,
And, around the dear ruin, each wish of my heart
Would entwine itself verdantly still.

It is not, while beauty and youth are thine own,
    And thy cheeks unprofan'd by a tear,
That the fervor and faith of a soul can be known,
    To which time will but make thee more dear!
No, the heart that has truly lov'd never forgets,
    But as truly loves on to the close,
As the sunflower turns on her god, when he sets
    The same look which she turn'd when he rose!

THOMAS MOORE

OH, NO – NOT EV' N WHEN WE FIRST LOV'D

Oh, no – not ev'n when first we lov'd
Wert thou as dear as now thou art;
Thy beauty then my senses mov'd
But now thy virtues bind my heart,
What was but Passion's sigh before
Has since been turn'd to Reason's vow;
And, though I then might love thee *more*,
Trust me, I love thee *better* now.

Although my heart in earlier youth
Might kindle with more wild desire,
Believe me, it has gain'd in truth
Much more than it has lost in fire.
The flame now warms my inmost core
That then but sparkled o'er my brow,
And though I seem'd to love thee more
Yet, oh, I love thee better now.

THOMAS MOORE

PHILIP MARLOWE'S TRANSLATION OF OVID'S ELEGIA 5

In summers heate and mid-time of the day
    To rest my limbes upon a bed I lay,
One window shut, the other open stood,
    Which gave such light as twinkles in a wood,
Like twilight glimpse at setting of the Sunne,
    Or night being past, and yet not day begunne.
Such light to shamefast maidens must be showne,
    Where they may sport, and seeme to be unknowne.
Then came Corinna in a long loose gowne,
    Her white neck hid with tresses hanging downe,
Resembling fayre Semiramis going to bed,
    Or Layis of a thousand lovers sped.
I snatcht her gowne: being thin, the harme was small,
    Yet strived she to be covered therewithall.

And striving thus as one that would be cast,
  Betrayde her selfe, and yeelded at the last.
Starke naked as she stood before mine eye,
  Not one wen in her body could I spie.
What armes and shoulders did I touch and see,
  How apt her breasts were to be prest by me.
How smooth a belly under her wast saw I,
  How large a legge, and what a lustie thigh?
To leave the rest, all liked me passing well,
  I clinged her naked body, downe she fell,
Judge you the rest, being tirde she bad me kisse;
  Jove send me more such after-noones as this.

OVID

ACROSS THE SKY

Across the sky the daylight crept,
And birds grew garrulous in the grove,
And on my marriage-morn I slept
A soft sleep undisturb'd by love.

COVENTRY PATMORE

TO HELEN

Helen, thy beauty is to me
Like those Nicèan barks of yore,
That gently, o'er a perfumed sea,
The weary, way-worn wanderer bore
To his own native shore.

On desperate seas long wont to roam,
Thy hyacinth hair, thy classic face,
Thy Naiad airs have brought me home
To the glory that was Greece,
And the grandeur that was Rome.

Lo! in yon brilliant window-niche
How statue-like I see thee stand,
The agate lamp within thy hand!
Ah! Psyche, from the regions which
Are Holy-Land!

EDGAR ALLAN POE

A LOVER'S FEAR

Like a musician that with flying finger
Startles the voice of some new instrument,
And though he know that in one string are blent
All its extremes of sound, yet still doth linger
Among the lighter threads, fearing to start
The deep soul of that one melodious wire,
Lest it, unanswering, dash his high desire,
And spoil the hopes of his expectant heart;
Thus my mistress oft conversing, I
Stir every lighter theme with careless voice,
Gathering sweet music and celestial joys
From the harmonious soul o'er which I fly;
Yet o'er the one deep master-chord I hover,
And dare not stoop, fearing to tell – I love her.

WILLIAM CALDWELL ROSCOE

SONNET II

I wish I could remember that
first day,
First hour, first moment of your
meeting me,
If bright or dim the season, it
might be
Summer or Winter for aught I
can say;
So unrecorded did it slip away,
So blind was I to see and to foresee,
So dull to mark the budding of
my tree
That would not blossom yet for
many a May.

If only I could recollect it, such
A day of days! I let it come and go
As traceless as a thaw of
bygone snow:
It seemed to mean so little, meant
so much;
If only now I could recall that touch,
First touch of hand in hand – Did
one but know!

CHRISTINA ROSSETTI

SONNET V

O my heart's heart and you who are to me
More than myself myself, God be with you,
Keep you in strong obedience, leal and true
To Him whose noble service setteth free;
Give you all good we see or can foresee,
Make your joys many and your sorrows few,
Bless you in what you bear and what you do,
Yea, perfect you as He would have you be.
So much for you; but what for me, dear friend?
To love you without stint and all I can
Today, tomorrow, world without an end;
To love you much, and yet to love you more,
As Jordan at its flood sweeps either shore;
Since woman is the helpmeet made for man.

CHRISTINA ROSSETTI

REMEMBER

Remember me when I am gone away,
Gone far away into the silent land;
When you can no more hold me by the hand,
Nor I half turn to go, yet turning stay.
Remember me when no more day by day
You tell me of our future that you planned:
Only remember me; you understand
It will be late to counsel then or pray.
Yet if you should forget me for a while
And afterwards remember, do not grieve:
For if the darkness and corruption leave
A vestige of thoughts that once I had,
Better by far you should forget and smile
Than that you should remember and be sad.

CHRISTINA ROSSETTI

SONNET XIV

Youth gone, and beauty gone if ever there
Dwelt beauty in so poor a face as this;
Youth gone and beauty, what remains of bliss?
I will not bind fresh roses in my hair,
To shame a cheek at best but little fair,—
Leave youth his roses, who can bear a thorn,—
I will not seek for blossoms anywhere,
Except such common flowers as blow with corn.
Youth gone and beauty gone, what doth remain?
The longing of a heart pent up forlorn,
A silent heart whose silence loves and longs;
The silence of a heart which sang its songs
While youth and beauty made a summer morn,
Silence of love that cannot sing again.

CHRISTINA ROSSETTI

SONG

When I am dead, my dearest,
  Sing no sad songs for me;
Plant thou no roses at my head,
  Nor shady cypress tree:
Be the green grass above me
With showers and dewdrops wet;
And if thou wilt, remember,
  And if thou wilt, forget.

I shall not see the shadows,
  I shall not feel the rain;
I shall not hear the nightingale
  Sing on, as if in pain:
And dreaming through the twilight
  That doth not rise nor set,
Haply I may remember,
  And haply may forget.

CHRISTINA ROSSETTI

SILENT NOON

Your hands lie open in the long fresh grass,
  The finger-points look through like rosy blooms:
Your eyes smile peace. The pasture gleams and glooms
  'Neath billowing skies that scatter and amass.

All round our nest, far as the eye can pass,
  Are golden kingcup-fields with silver edge
Where the cow-parsley skirts the hawthorn-hedge.
  'Tis visible silence still as the hourglass.

Deep in the sun-searched growths the dragonfly
Hangs like a blue thread loosened from the sky:

So this wing'd hour is dropt to us from above
Oh! clasp we to our hearts, for deathless dower,
This close-companioned inarticulate hour
When twofold silence was the song of love.

DANTE GABRIEL ROSSETTI

SUDDEN LIGHT

I have been here before,
But when or how I cannot tell:
I know the grass beyond the door,
The sweet keen smell,
The sighing sound, the lights around the shore.

You have been mine before,—
How long ago I may not know:
But just when at that swallow's soar
Your neck turned so,
Some veil did fall, – I knew it all of yore.

Has this been thus before?
And shall not thus time's eddying flight
Still with our lives our love restore
In death's despite,
And day and night yield one delight once more?

DANTE GABRIEL ROSSETTI

WILLOWWOOD

I sat with Love upon a woodside well,
    Leaning across the water, I and he;
    Nor ever did he speak nor looked at me,
But touched his lute wherein was audible
The certain secret thing he had to tell:
    Only our mirrored eyes met silently
In the low wave; and that sound came to be
The passionate voice I knew; and my tears fell.

And at their fall, his eyes beneath grew hers;
    And with his foot and with his wing feathers
He swept the spring that watered my heart's drouth.
    Then the dark ripples spread to waving hair,
    And as I stooped, her own lips rising there
Bubbled with brimming kisses at my mouth.

DANTE GABRIEL ROSSETTI

from CYRANO DE BERGERAC

A kiss, when all is said, what is it?
An oath that's given closer than before;
A promise more precise; the sealing of
Confessions that till then were barely breathed;
A rosy dot placed on the 'i' in loving;
A secret that is confined to a mouth and not to ears.

EDMOND ROSTAND

Let the lover be disgraceful, crazy,
absent minded. Someone sober
will worry about things going badly.
Let the lover be.

RUMI

from **THIEF OF SLEEP**

Suddenly the drunken sweetheart appeared out
of my door.
She drank a cup of ruby wine and sat by my side.
Seeing and holding the lockets of her hair
My face became all eyes, and my eyes all hands.

RUMI

THE FRESHNESS

When it's cold and raining,
you are more beautiful.

And the snow brings me
even closer to your lips.

The inner secret, that which was never born,
you are that freshness, and I am with
you now.

I can't explain the goings,
or the comings. You enter suddenly,

and I am nowhere again.
Inside the majesty.

RUMI

FRAGMENT 31

That man seems to me to be like a god, to
Sit so close to you and to hear your sweet voice
And your charming laughter – and all this, truly,
Makes my heart tremble;

For I only, briefly, need glance at you to
Find my voice has gone and my tongue is broken,
And a flame has stolen beneath my skin, my
Eyes can no longer

See, my ears are ringing, while drops of sweat run
Down my trembling body, and I've turned paler
Than a wisp of straw and it seems to me I'm
Not far off dying.

SAPPHO

THE LAY OF THE LAST MINSTREL

And said I that my limbs were old;
And said I that my blood was cold,
And that my kindly fire was fled,
And my poor withered heart was dead,
And that I might not sing of love?
How could I to the dearest theme,
That ever warmed a minstrel's dream,
So foul, so false, a recreant prove!
How could I name love's very name
Nor wake my harp to notes of flame!

In peace, Love tunes the shepherd's reed;
In war, he mounts the warrior's steed;
In halls, in gay attire is seen;
In hamlets, dances on the green.
Love rules the court, the camp, the grove,
And men below, and saints above;
For love is heaven, and heaven is love.

SIR WALTER SCOTT

THE PROPHECY

'The rose is fairest when 'tis budding new,
And hope is brightest when it dawns from fears:
The rose is sweetest wash'd with morning dew,
And love is loveliest when embalm'd in tears.
O wilding rose, whom fancy thus endears,
I bid your blossoms in my bonnet wave,
Emblem of hope and love through future years!'
Thus spoke young Norman, heir of Armandave,
What time the sun arose on Vennachar's broad wave.

SIR WALTER SCOTT

TO CLORIS

Cloris, I cannot say your eyes
Did my unwary heart surprise;
Nor will I swear it was your face,
Your shape, or any nameless grace:
For you are so entirely fair,
To love a part, injustice were;
No drowning man can know which drop
Of water his last breath did stop;
So when the stars in heaven appear,
And join to make the night look clear;
The light we no one's bounty call,
But the obliging gift of all.
He that does lips or hands adore,
Deserves them only, and no more;
But I love all, and every part,
And nothing less can ease my heart.
Cupid, that lover, weakly strikes,
Who can express what 'tis he likes.

SIR CHARLES SEDLEY

SONNET 116

Let me not to the marriage of
true minds
Admit impediments. Love is
not love
Which alters when it
alteration finds,
Or bends with the remover
to remove:
O, no; it is an ever-fixed mark,
That looks on tempests and is
never shaken;
It is the star to every
wandering bark,
Whose worth's unknown, although
his height be taken.

Love's not Time's fool, though rosy
lips and cheeks
Within his bending sickle's
compass come;
Love alters not with his brief hours
and weeks,
But bears it out even to the edge
of doom.
If this be error and upon me prov'd,
I never writ, nor no man ever lov'd.

WILLIAM SHAKESPEARE

SONNET 120

That time of year thou may'st in me behold
When yellow leaves, or none, or few, do hang
Upon those boughs which shake against the cold,
Bare ruined choirs, where late the sweet birds sang.
In me thou see'st the twilight of such day
As after sunset fadeth in the west;
Which by and by black night doth take away,
Death's second self, that seals up all in rest.
In me thou see'st the glowing of such fire,
That on the ashes of his youth doth lie,
As the death-bed whereon it must expire,
Consumed with that which it was nourished by.
This thou perceiv'st, which makes thy love more strong,
To love that well which thou must leave ere long.

WILLIAM SHAKESPEARE

SONNET 51

Thus can my love excuse the slow offence
Of my dull bearer, when from thee I speed:
From where thou art, why should I haste me thence?
Till I return, of posting is no need.
O, what excuse will my poor beast then find,
When swift extremity can seem but slow?
Then should I spur, though mounted on the wind,
In wingèd speed no motion shall I know:
Then can no horse with my desire keep pace;
Therefore desire, of perfect'st love being made
Shall neigh – no dull flesh – in his fiery race;
But love, for love, thus shall excuse my jade;
Since from thee going he went willful-slow,
Towards thee I'll run and give him leave to go.

WILLIAM SHAKESPEARE

SONNET 55

Not marble, nor the gilded monuments
Of princes, shall outlive this powerful rhyme;
But you shall shine more bright in these contents
Than unswept stone, besmear'd with sluttish time.
When wasteful war shall statues overturn,
And broils root out the work of masonry,
Nor Mars his sword nor war's quick fire shall burn
The living record of your memory.
'Gainst death and all-oblivious enmity
Shall you pace forth; your praise shall still find room
Even in the eyes of all posterity
That wear this world out to the ending doom.
So, till the judgement that yourself arise,
You live in this, and dwell in lovers' eyes.

WILLIAM SHAKESPEARE

SONNET 75

So are you to my thoughts as food to life,
Or as sweet-season'd showers are to the ground;
And for the peace of you I hold such strife
As 'twixt a miser and his wealth is found;
Now proud as an enjoyer, and anon
Doubting the filching age will steal his treasure;
Now counting best to be with you alone,
Then better'd that the world may see my pleasure:
Sometime all full with feasting on your sight,
And by and by clean starved for a look;
Possessing or pursuing no delight,
Save what is had or must from you be took.
Thus do I pine and surfeit day by day,
Or gluttoning on all, or all away.

WILLIAM SHAKESPEARE

SONNET 14

Not from the stars do I my judgement pluck;
And yet methinks I have astronomy,
But not to tell of good or evil luck,
Of plagues, of dearths, or seasons' quality;
Nor can I fortune to brief minutes tell,
Pointing to each his thunder, rain and wind,
Or say with princes if it shall go well,
By oft predict that I in heaven find:
But from thine eyes my knowledge I derive,
And, constant stars, in them I read such art,
As truth and beauty shall together thrive,
If from thyself to store thou wouldst convert;
Or else of thee this I prognosticate:
Thy end is truth's and beauty's doom and date.

WILLIAM SHAKESPEARE

SONNET 18

Shall I compare thee to a summer's day?
Thou art more lovely and more temperate:
Rough winds do shake the darling buds of May,
And summer's lease hath all too short a date:
Sometime too hot the eye of heaven shines,
And often is his gold complexion dimm'd;
And every fair from fair sometime declines,
By chance or nature's changing course untrimm'd;
But thy eternal summer shall not fade,
Nor lose possession of that fair thou ow'st;
Nor shall Death brag thou wander'st in his shade,
When in eternal lines to time thou grow'st;
So long as men can breathe, or eyes can see,
So long lives this, and this gives life to thee.

WILLIAM SHAKESPEARE

SONNET 26

Lord of my love, to whom in vassalage
Thy merit hath my duty strongly knit.
To thee I send this written embassage,
To witness duty, not to show my wit:
Duty so great, which wit so poor as mine
May make seem bare, in wanting words to show it,
But that I hope some good conceit of thine
In thy soul's thought, all naked, will bestow it
Till whatsoever star that guides my moving,
Points on me graciously with fair aspect,
And puts apparel on my tatter'd loving,
To show me worthy of thy sweet respect:
Then may I dare to boast how I do love thee;
Till then not show my head where thou mayst prove me.

WILLIAM SHAKESPEARE

WHEN PASSION'S TRANCE IS OVERPAST

When passion's trance is overpast,
If tenderness and truth could last,
Or live, whilst all wild feelings keep
Some mortal slumber, dark and deep,
I should not weep, I should not weep!

It were enough to feel, to see,
Thy soft eyes gazing tenderly,
And dream the rest – and burn and be
The secret food of fires unseen,
Couldst thou but be as thou hast been.

After the slumber of the year
The woodland violets reappear;
All things revive in field or grove,
And sky and sea, but two, which move
And form all others – life, and love.

PERCY BYSSHE SHELLEY

from THE ARABIC: AN IMITATION

My faint spirit was sitting in
the light
Of thy looks, my love;
It panted for thee like the hind
at noon
For the brooks, my love.
The barb whose hoofs outspeed the
tempest's flight
Bore thee far from me;
My heart, for my weak feet were
weary soon,
Did companion thee.

Ah! fleeter far than fleetest storm
or steed,
Or the death they bear,
The heart which tender thought
clothes like a dove
With the wings of care;
In the battle, in the darkness, in
the need,
Shall mine cling to thee,
Nor claim one smile for all the
comfort, love,
It may bring to thee.

PERCY BYSSHE SHELLEY

LOVE'S PHILOSOPHY

The Fountains mingle with the River
And the Rivers with the Ocean,
The winds of Heaven mix for ever
With a sweet emotion;
Nothing in the world is single;
All things by a law divine
In one spirit meet and mingle.
Why not I with thine?—

See the mountains kiss high Heaven
And the waves clasp one another;
No sister-flower would be forgiven
If it disdained its brother,
And the sunlight clasps the earth
And the moonbeams kiss the sea:
What is all this sweet work worth
If thou kiss not me?

PERCY BYSSHE SHELLEY

TO —

One word is too often profaned
For me to profane it,
One feeling too falsely disdained
For thee to disdain it.
One hope is too like despair
For prudence to smother,
And pity from thee more dear
Than that from another.

I can give not what men call love,
But wilt thou accept not
The worship the heart lifts above
And the Heavens reject not,—
The desire of the moth for the star,
Of the night for the morrow,
The devotion to something afar
From the sphere of our sorrow?

PERCY BYSSHE SHELLEY

TO —

Music, when soft voices die,
    Vibrates in the memory—
Odours, when sweet violets sicken,
Live within the sense they quicken.

Rose leaves, when the rose is dead,
    Are heaped for the belovèd's bed;
And so thy thoughts, when thou art gone,
    Love itself shall slumber on.

PERCY BYSSHE SHELLEY

THE BARGAIN

My true love hath my heart, and I have his,
    By just exchange one for another given:
I hold his dear, and mine he cannot miss,
    There never was a better bargain driven:
My true love hath my heart, and I have his.

My heart in me keeps him and me in one,
My heart in him his thoughts and senses guides:
    He loves my heart, for once it was his own,
    I cherish his because in me it bides:
My true love hath my heart, and I have his.

SIR PHILIP SIDNEY

SONNET FIVE, *from* ASTROPHEL AND STELLA

It is most true, that eyes are form'd to serve
The inward light; and that the heavenly part
Ought to be king, from whose rules who do swerve,
Rebels to Nature, strive for their own smart.
It is most true, what we call Cupid's dart,
An image is, which for ourselves we carve:
And, fools, adore in temple of our heart,
Till that good God make Church and churchman starve.
True, that true Beauty Virtue is indeed,
Whereof this Beauty can be but a shade,
Which elements with mortal mixture breed:
True, that on earth we are but pilgrims made,
And should in soul up to our country move:
True, and yet true that I must Stella love.

SIR PHILIP SIDNEY

THE GARDEN OF BEAUTY

Coming to kiss her lips (such grace I found),
Me seem'd I smelt a garden of sweet flow'rs
That dainty odours from them threw around,
For damsels fit to deck their lovers' bow'rs.
Her lips did smell like unto gilliflowers,
Her ruddy cheeks like unto roses red,
Her snowy brows like budded bellamoures,
Her lovely eyes like pinks but newly spread,
Her goodly bosom like a strawberry bed,
Her neck like to a bunch of cullambines,
Her breast like lilies ere their leaves be shed,
Her nipples like young blossom'd jessamines:
Such fragrant flow'rs do give most odourous smell,
But her sweet odour did them all excel.

EDMUND SPENSER

LOVE IN ABSENCE

Like as the culver on the barèd bough
Sits mourning for the absence of her mate,
And in her songs sends many a wishful vow
For his return, that seems to linger late;
So I alone, now left disconsolate,
Mourn to myself the absence of my love,
And wandering here and there all desolate,
Seek with my plaints to match that mournful dove.
No joy of ought that under heaven doth hove
Can comfort me, but her own joyous sight,
Whose sweet aspect both God and man can move,
In her unspotted pleasance to delight:
Dark is my day whiles her fair light I miss,
And dead my life, that wants such lively bliss.

EDMUND SPENSER

MY LOVE IS LIKE TO ICE

My Love is like to ice, and I to fire:
How comes it then that this her cold so great
Is not dissolved through my so hot desire,
But harder grows the more I her entreat?
Or how comes it that my exceeding heat
Is not allayed by her heart – frozen cold,

But that I burn much more in boiling sweat,
And feel my flames augmented manifold?
What more miraculous thing may be told,
That fire, which all things melts, should harden ice,
And ice, which is congeal'd with senseless cold,
Should kindle fire by wonderful device?
Such is the power of love in gentle mind,
That it can alter all the course of kind.

EDMUND SPENSER

MY WIFE

Trusty, dusky, vivid, true,
With eyes of gold and bramble-dew,
Steel-true and blade-straight,
The great artificer
Made my mate.

Honour, anger, valour, fire;
A love that life could never tire,
Death quench or evil stir,
The mighty master
Gave to her.

Teacher, tender comrade, wife,
A fellow-farer true through life,
Heart-whole and soul-free
The august father
Gave to me.

ROBERT LOUIS STEVENSON

THE STOLEN HEART

I prythee send me back my heart
Since I cannot have thine;
For if from yours you will not part,
Why then shouldst thou have mine?

Yet now I think on't, let it lie;
To find it were in vain,
For thou'st a thief in either eye
Would steal it back again.

Why should two hearts in one breast lie,
And yet not lodge together?
O love! where is thy sympathy,
If thus our breasts you sever?

But love is such a mystery,
I cannot find it out;
For when I think I'm best resolved
I then am most in doubt.

Then farewell love, and farewell woe,
I will no longer pine;
For I'll believe I have her heart
As much as she hath mine.

SIR JOHN SUCKLING

ON STELLA'S BIRTHDAY

Stella this day is thirty-four,
(We won't dispute a year or more),
However Stella, be not troubled,
Although thy size and years are doubled,
Since first I saw thee at sixteen
The brightest virgin on the green,
So little is thy form declin'd
Made up so largely in thy mind.
Oh, would it please the Gods to split
Thy beauty, size, and years, and wit,
No age could furnish out a pair
Of nymphs so graceful, wise and fair
With half the lustre of your eyes,
With half thy wit, thy years and size:
And then before it grew too late,
How should I beg of gentle Fate
(That either nymph might have her swain)
To split my worship too in twain.

JONATHAN SWIFT

OBLATION

Ask nothing more of me, sweet;
  All I can give you I give.
Heart of my heart, were it more,
More would be laid at your feet:
Love that should help you to live,—
Song that should spur you to soar.

All things were nothing to give,
Once to have sense of you more,—
Touch you and taste of you, sweet,
Think you and breathe you and live
Swept of your wings as they soar,
  Trodden by chance of your feet.

I, that have love and no more,
Bring you but love of you, sweet.
He that hath more, let him give;
He that hath wings, let him soar,
  Mine is the heart at your feet
Here, that must love you to live.

ALGERNON CHARLES SWINBURNE

LIKE THE TOUCH OF RAIN

Like the touch of rain she was
On a man's flesh and hair and eyes
When the joy of walking thus
Has taken him by surprise:

With the love of the storm he burns,
He sings, he laughs, well I know how,
But forgets when he returns
As I shall not forget her 'Go now.'

Those two shut a door
Between me and the blessed rain
That was never shut before
And will not open again.

EDWARD THOMAS

Come here, my love, the crown of my home—
Walking so tall, so slender, like a cypress,
With your black hair falling to your feet,
With brows like a tightened bow;
With a mouth too small for two almonds
And cheeks red like the apples of autumn—
My woman, my lady, my love.

TURKISH TRIBAL CHIEFTAIN

SONNET UPON A STOLEN KISS

Now gentle sleep hath closèd up those eyes
Which, waking, kept my boldest thoughts in awe;
And free access unto that sweet lip lies,
From whence I long the rosy breath to draw.
Methinks no wrong it were, if I should steal
From those two melting rubies one poor kiss;
None sees the theft that would the theft reveal,
Nor rob I her of aught what she can miss:
Nay, should I twenty kisses take away,
There would be little sign I would do so;
Why then should I this robbery delay?
O, she may awake and therewith angry grow!
Well, if she do, I'll back restore that one,
And twenty hundred thousand more for loan.

GEORGE WITHER

SURPRISED BY JOY

Surprised by joy – impatient as the Wind
I turned to share the transport – Oh! with whom
But Thee, deep buried in the silent tomb,
That spot which no vicissitude can find?
Love, faithful love, recalled thee to my mind—
But how could I forget thee? Through what power,
Even for the least division of an hour,
Have I been so beguiled as to be blind
To my most grievous loss! – That thought's return
Was the worst pang that sorrow ever bore,
Save one, one only, when I stood forlorn,
Knowing my heart's best treasure was no more;
That neither present time, nor years unborn
Could to my sight that heavenly face restore.

WILLIAM WORDSWORTH

YES! THOU ART FAIR

Yes! thou art fair, yet be not moved
To scorn the declaration,
That sometimes I in thee have loved
My fancy's own creation.

Imagination needs must stir;
Dear Maid, this truth believe,
Minds that have nothing to confer
Find little to perceive.

Be pleased that nature made thee fit
To feed my heart's devotion,
By laws to which all Forms submit
In sky, air, earth, and ocean.

WILLIAM WORDSWORTH

WHAT HEAVENLY SMILES!

What heavenly smiles! O Lady mine
Through my very heart they shine;
And, if my brow gives back their light,
Do thou look gladly on the sight;
As the clear Moon with modest pride
Beholds her own bright beams.
Reflected from the mountain's side
And from the headlong streams.

WILLIAM WORDSWORTH

TO —

Let other bards of angels sing,
Bright suns without a spot;
But thou art no such perfect thing:
Rejoice that thou art not!

Heed not tho' none should call thee fair:
So, Mary, let it be
If naught in loveliness compare
With what thou art to me.

True beauty dwells in deep retreats,
Whose veil is unremoved
Till heart with heart in concord beats,
And the lover is beloved.

WILLIAM WORDSWORTH

BEHOLD, LOVE, THY POWER

Behold, Love, thy power how she despiseth!
My grevious pain how little she regardeth!
The solemn oath, whereof she taketh no cure,
    Broken she hath; and yet she bideth sure
Right at her ease and little thee she dreadeth.
Weaponed thou art, and she unarmèd sitteth;
    To thee disdainful, all her life she leadeth,
    To me spiteful without cause or measure,
    Behold, love, how proudly she triumpteth.

    I am in hold: if thee pity moveth,
Go, bend thy bow, that stony hearts breaketh,
And with some stroke revenge the displeasure
    Of thee, and him that sorrow doth endure,
And, as his lord, the lowly here entreateth.
    Behold, love.

SIR THOMAS WYATT

A RENOUNCING OF LOVE

Farewell, Love, and all thy laws forever.
Thy baited hooks shall tangle me no more.
Senec and Plato call me from thy lore,
To perfect wealth my wit for to endeavour.
In blind error when I did persever,
Thy sharp repulse, that pricketh ay so sore,
Hath taught me to set in trifles no store,
And scape forth, since liberty is lever.
Therefore, farewell: Go trouble younger hearts.
And in me claim no more authority.
With idle youth go use thy property,
And thereon spend thy many brittle darts;
For hitherto though I have lost all my time,
Me lusteth no longer rotten boughs to climb.

SIR THOMAS WYATT

A DRINKING SONG

Wine comes in at the mouth
And love comes in at the eye;
That's all we know for truth
Before we grow old and die.
I lift the glass to my mouth,
I look at you, and I sigh.

W. B. YEATS

BROWN PENNY

I whispered, 'I am too young,'
And then, 'I am old enough';
Wherefore I threw a penny
To find out if I might love.
'Go and love, go and love, young man,
If the lady be young and fair.'
Ah, penny, brown penny, brown penny,
I am looped in the loops of her hair.

O love is the crooked thing,
There is nobody wise enough
To find out all that is in it,
For he would be thinking of love
Till the stars had run away
And the shadows eaten the moon.
Ah, penny, brown penny, brown penny,
One cannot begin it too soon.

W. B. YEATS

THE PITY OF LOVE

A pity beyond all telling
Is hid in the heart of love:
The folk who are buying and selling,
The clouds on their journey above,
The cold, wet winds ever blowing,
And the shadowy hazel grove
Where mouse-grey waters are flowing
Threaten the head that I love.

W. B. YEATS

YOU'RE THE SPRING IN MY STEP

ISBN: 978-1-84953-517-5

Hardback

£5.99

Falling in love is like finding the yin to your yang, the butter on your crumpet, the Holmes to your Watson. This little book is packed with romantic, funny and charming ways to tell the one you love just how much they mean to you.

If you're interested in finding out more about our books, find us on Facebook at Summersdale Publishers and follow us on Twitter at @Summersdale.

www.summersdale.com